First World War
and Army of Occupation
War Diary
France, Belgium and Germany

57 DIVISION
172 Infantry Brigade
King's (Liverpool Regiment)
2/10 Battalion
10 September 1915 - 24 February 1916

WO95/2985/5

The Naval & Military Press Ltd
www.nmarchive.com
Published in association with The National Archives

Published by

The Naval & Military Press Ltd

Unit 10 Ridgewood Industrial Park,

Uckfield, East Sussex,

TN22 5QE England

Tel: +44 (0) 1825 749494

www.naval-military-press.com

www.nmarchive.com

This diary has been reprinted in facsimile from the original. Any imperfections are inevitably reproduced and the quality may fall short of modern type and cartographic standards.

© Crown Copyright
Images reproduced by permission of The National Archives, London, England, 2015.

Contents

Document type	Place/Title	Date From	Date To
Heading	WO95/2985/5 57 Divn 172 Inf Brig 2/10 King's Liverpool Regt 1915 Aug-1916 Feb		
Heading	War Diary 2/10th (Scottish) Battalion The King's (Liverpool Regiment) Tandridge Camp Oxted Surrey Period September 1st To September 30th 1915		
Miscellaneous	War Diary August 1915		
War Diary	Oxted Surrey	10/09/1915	30/09/1915
Heading	2/10th (Scottish) Battalion "The King's" Liverpool Regiment War Diary From October 1st 1915 To October 31st 1915		
War Diary	Oxted	05/10/1915	23/10/1915
War Diary	Maidstone	30/10/1915	30/10/1915
Heading	War Diary And Summary Of Events And Information Headquarters 2/10th Bn. King's Liverpool Regiment. Period November 1st 1915 to November 30th 1915.		
War Diary	Maidstone	01/11/1915	26/11/1915
Heading	War Diary 2/10th (Scottish) Battalion The King's (Liverpool Regt) December 1st 1915 To December 31st 1915		
War Diary	Maidstone	02/12/1915	30/12/1915
War Diary	War Diary Headquarters 2/10th (Scottish) Bn. King's Liverpool Regt Station Maidstone Kent Period January 1916 And Summary of Events and Information		
War Diary	Maidstone	16/01/1916	30/01/1916
Heading	2/10th (Scottish) Bn. L'pool Regt War Diary For The Month Of February 1916		
War Diary	Maidstone	04/02/1916	24/02/1916

WO 95 2955/5

57 Div.; 172 Inf Brig.
2/10 King's Liverpool Regt
1915 Aug - 1916 Feb

172 BDE

WAR DIARY

2/10th (Scottish) Battalion The King's (Liverpool Regiment).

TANDRIDGE CAMP,
OXTED, SURREY.

Period

September 1st to September 30th 1915.

and

Summary of Events and Information

Tandridge Camp,
Oxted, Surrey.
6th October 1915.

WAR DIARY - AUGUST 1915.

2/10th (Scottish) Bn. King's Liverpool Regt.

MONTHLY SUMMARY OF EVENTS AND INFORMATION.

UNIT. 2/10th (Scottish) Battn. King's Liverpool Regiment.

BRIGADE. 172nd Infantry Brigade. T.F.

DIVISION. 57th (West Lancashire) Division, T.F.

ORGANIZATION FOR DEFENCE. Part of 2nd Army.

TEMPORARY WAR STATION. Ashford, Kent, until 22nd August, 1915.
Oxted, Surrey, from 25th August, 1915.

MOBILIZATION WAR STATION.)
ADMINISTRATIVE CENTRE.) L I V E R P O O L.

THIRD LINE DEPOT. Weeton Camp, Nr. Preston.

FORMATION. Battalion Constitute.

TRAINING. The training has been carried out during the month according to programme, which included entrenching by day and night, instruction in bomb throwing, assaults on trenches and consolidation of trenches when captured, Bayonet Fighting, attack, defence, outpost practices, construction of portable and fixed wire entanglements, musketry instruction.
The machine gun and Signalling Sections and Scouts carried out training under their Instructors.

DISCIPLINE. Has been excellent.

REINFORCEMENTS FOR LINKED BATTALION. One Captain was sent as reinforcement but no drafts were called for.

MUSKETRY. .303 Rifles are urgently wanted for training the 809 Recruits, and for firing the General Musketry Course by 54 Recruits, who have undergone preliminary training Musketry.

ENTRENCHING. Sandbags are urgently needed for instructional purposes.

TRANSPORT. Horses are urgently needed to enable the Transport Section to be trained and also for horsing wagons.

CLOTHING. If Kilts could be obtained for the Recruits it would greatly encourage them and improve the appearance of the Battalion.

Adam Lawrie

Cdg. 2/10th (Scottish) Bn. The King's (Liverpool Regt.)

Army Form C. 2118

2/10th (Scottish) Bn. The King's ((L'pool Regt.))

WAR DIARY
or
INTELLIGENCE SUMMARY
(Erase heading not required.)

Instructions regarding War Diaries and Intelligence Summaries are contained in F. S. Regs., Part II. and the Staff Manual respectively. Title Pages will be prepared in manuscript.

Place	Date	Hour	Summary of Events and Information	Remarks and references to Appendices
OXTED SURREY.	1915 10.9.		Capt. R.H.D.Lockhart joined for Light Duty having been on Sick Furlough since 28/2/15.	
	10.9.		Sec.Lieut. A.K.Ferguson joined for duty.	
	18.9.		Sec.Lieut. A.S.Darroch joined for duty.	
	19.9.		Sec.Lieut. J.H.Bradley,9th E.York.Regt.Sec.Lt.H.S.Bennet,10th Border Regt.) Joined for duty	
	"		" " L.E.Cole 11th K.O.Y.L.I. Sec.Lt.J.H.Thornton,10th " ") and	
	"		" " E.S.Wright,10th Border Regt.) training.	
	21.9.		Sec:Lieut. J.C.Belford,13th W.York.Regt.Sec.Lt. T.A.Whitehead,13th W.York. -do-	
	23.9.		" Lieuts.J.R.MacSwiney,G.M.Morris, S.R.Lewis & A.M.Morris joined for duty.	
	24.9.		" Lieut. E.H.Gatton, 9th Lincoln Regt. joined for duty and training.	
	27.9.		Captain D.A.Bingham,Sec.Lts. A.H.Noble, R.T.Ainsworth, F.Davey & H.L.Woodland proceeded as re-inforcements for First Battalion overseas.	
	27.9.		Sec"Lt. N.Mather joined for duty.	
	27.9.	11.17 p.m:-	A Brigade Parctice Night Alarm was held. The Alarm was received at 10.45 p.m. The Battalion was on parade at 11.17 p.m:-	
			57 Officers, 492 other ranks, Machine Gun, 2 G.S.Wagons carrying 16 boxes .250 S.A.A. each. 1 G.S.Wagon carrying 40 picks and 40 shovels. 1 M.O. Cart. 1 single cart carrying forage. 1 A.S.C. S.S. Wagon carrying 50 picks and 50 shovels. 1 A.S.C. GWS.Wagon carrying Camp Kettles and Cooks gear, 1 A.S.C. G.S.Wagon carrying Rations. 1 G.S.Wagon carrying 8 Boxes.303 M.G.Amn. 5 Horses Riding, 9 Mules Pack, 11 Horses Draught. 1 Horse spare.	
	30.9.		2nd Lieut. G.D.Morton left as re-inforcement for First Battalion overseas.	
	30.9.	9.19.	A Practice Day Alarm was held. Alarm sent out 8.53. Battalion on parade:-First Coy.9.19. last Company 9.19. Strength 38 Officers 453 other ranks.	
			Horses riding 7. Horses Draught 7. 3 G.S.Wagons. 1 M.O.Cart.	

Odam Lawrie ....Lt-Col.
Commanding.
2/10th (Scottish) Bn. The King's (L'pool Regt.)

2/10th. (Scottish) Battalion "The King's" Liverpool
Regiment.

WAR   DIARY

from October 1st. 1915.
to October 31st. 1915.

Army Form C. 2118.

WAR DIARY
or
INTELLIGENCE SUMMARY.
(Erase heading not required.)

Instructions regarding War Diaries and Intelligence Summaries are contained in F.S. Regs., Part II. and the Staff Manual respectively. Title pages will be prepared in manuscript.

Place	Date 1915	Hour	Summary of Events and Information	Remarks and references to Appendices
Oxted	5/10		Sec.Lieut.A.H.Bellis joined for duty.	
	8/10		Sec.Lieut.E.H.Hollins and Sec.Lieut.L.B.Mill proceeded as re-inforcements for Battn. Overseas.	
	10/10		Sec.Lieut.T.A.Roberts joined for duty.	
	12/10		Sec.Lieut.R.J.McKinnell joined from Sick Leave.	
	12/10		Sec.Lieut.W.O.Stott, 16th Bn.L'pool Regt. left the station to rejoin his regiment.	
	16/10		Sec.Lieut.S.W.Hodgson joined for duty.	
	18/10		Sec.Lieut.L.Barnish joined for duty.	
	25/10		Sec.Lieuts J.Grant, J.E.Cookson, D.McIntyre, and A.Jowett joined for duty.	
	13/10		Two Zeppelins came round the Battalion's lines, and on being fired at by the Brigade Machine Gun Officer, turned and came over the lines, but did not drop any bombs.	
	21/10		A billeting party of 4 N.C.O.'s under Lt.A.Cookson left the station and proceeded to Maidstone as a billeting party.	
			An advance party of 1 Sergt. 1 Corpl., and 12men left the station and proceeded to Maidstone.	
	22/10		A Brigade practice night alarm was held. The alarm was received at 10-45 pm., the first company was on parade by 11-14 pm and the last company at 11-29 pm. On parade:- 31 officers, 523 other ranks.	
	23/10		Change of Station. The battalion marched off at 10-30 am on change of station to Maidstone. On the first day's march from Oxted to Seal no men fell out. The battalion arrived at Seal at 3-15 pm, and halted for the night. One attached officer and one Band boy were left at Seal, sick. On the second day's march two men fell out. The battalion marched off at 8-10 am and arrived at Maidstone at 2-10 pm.	

	Officers	Other ranks
By Road	29	593
fell out	1	2
Advance parties	2	52
By Motors. (Rear Parties)	3	53
	35	680

Transport. 14 officers' horses. 39 light draught. 9 heavy draught. 1 machine gun. 10 wagons. 4 carts.

| Maidstone. | 30/10 | | A practice day alarm was held. The alarm was sent out at 9-15 am. First Company paraded at 9-42 am. Last Company paraded at 9-48 am. Transport-10-9 am Strength 29 officers, and 429 other ranks. | |

Adam Seann

1577 Wt.W10791/1773 500,000 1/15 D.D.& L. A.D.S.S./Forms/C. 2118.

WAR DIARY

and

SUMMARY OF EVENTS AND INFORMATION

Headquarters
2/10th.Bn. King's Liverpool Regiment

PERIOD

November 1st 1915

to

November 30th.1915.

3 Rocky Hill Terrace
Maidstone
December 4th.1915.

Army Form C. 2118.

WAR DIARY
or
INTELLIGENCE SUMMARY.
(Erase heading not required.)

Place	Date	Hour	Summary of Events and Information	Remarks and references to Appendices
Maidstone	1915			
	1/11/		Sec.Lieut. P.Carnelly joined for duty.	
	2/11/		Mr. R.S.Kemble joined for duty having been attached pending Gazette.	
	15/11/		Sec.Lt.D.McIntyre transferred to 3rd Line Depot.Authy:-W.O.L.9/8/435(T.F.3)dated 6/11/15.	
	22/11/		Sec.Lieuts.A.J.Graham, C.R.Taylor, R.S.Kemble, R.V.Clarke, A.K.Ferguson, J.R.McSwiney, J.R.McKinnell, N.E.Swindells, S.W.Hodgson, were transferred to 3rd Line Depot. (Authority:- War Office Letter 9/Infantry/ 2/T.F.3 dated 8th November, 1915.	
	22/11/		Sec.Lt. M.Steele left on transfer to 49th Provisional Battalion. (Authority:- C.R.W.C.88193/1.M.S. dated 8th November,1915.	
	23/11/15.		Lieut.A.T.Salvidge and Sec.Lieut.E.K.Glazebrook left the Station to proceed as reinforcements for First Battalion overseas.	
	26/11/15.		Sec.Lieut.N.Mather and S.R.Lewis were transferred to 3rd Line Depot. (Authority:- War Office Letter 9/Infantry/ 2/T.F.3. dated 8th November, 1915.	

Adam Lawrie

.... Lt. Col.
Odg. 2/10th (Scottish) Bn. The King's (L'pool Regt.)

WAR DIARY

by

2/10th (Scottish) Battalion The King&s (Liverpool Regt)

December 1st 1915

to

December 31st 1915

MAIDSTONE

5th January 1916.

Army Form C. 2118.

WAR DIARY
or
INTELLIGENCE SUMMARY.

(Erase heading not required.)

Instructions regarding War Diaries and Intelligence Summaries are contained in F. S. Regs., Part II. and the Staff Manual respectively. Title pages will be prepared in manuscript.

Place	Date 1915.	Hour	Summary of Events and Information	Remarks and references to Appendices
Maidstone	2.12		17 other ranks, Home service bandsmen and pipers left the Station to join 49th Provisional Battn.	A 8
	6-12		Sec.Lieut.E.H.Catton, attached from training and duty, left to join Royal Flying Corps.	A 8
	6-12		Death of No.4434 Bandman John Macdonald in Southern Hospital, Liverpool - illness.	A 8
	13-12		The Brass Band, consisting of 39 other ranks left to join 3rd Line at Blackpool.	A 8
	15-12		The G.O.C. 11 Army C.F. inspected the Battalion.	A 8
	18/12		52 other ranks, declared by Medical Board as fit for Service at Home only, left to join 49th Provisional Battalion at Norwich.	A 8
	21-12		The G. O. C. 57th (W.Lancs.) Divn. inspected the Battalion in an Outpost Scheme.	A 8
	30-12		Inspection of the Battalion in Musketry by Commandant, School of Musketry, Hythe.	A 8

Cam Savin
Lieut. Col.
Commanding
2/10th (Scottish) Battn. K.L.R.

War Diary

Headquarters

2/10th (Scottish) Bn. King's Liverpool Regt.

Station   Maidstone, Kent

Period   January 1916

— and —

Summary of Events and Information

Army Form C. 2118.

WAR DIARY
or
INTELLIGENCE SUMMARY.
(Erase heading not required.)

Instructions regarding War Diaries and Intelligence Summaries are contained in F.S. Regs., Part II. and the Staff Manual respectively. Title pages will be prepared in manuscript.

Place	Date	Hour	Summary of Events and Information	Remarks and references to Appendices
Maid-stone.	1916			
	16/1/16		Capt. W.J.H.Renison's appointment as Adjutant cancelled and the Officer transferred to 3rd Line.	
	19/1/16		Capt. C.B.Glynn transferred from 3rd Line, joined for Duty.	
	19/1/16		Capt. K.F. Wilson seconded for duty with a provisional Battalion. Left to join 49th Provisional Battalion at Norwich.	
	21/1/16		A draft of 14 recruits received from Administrative Centre.	
	22/1/16		A draft of 18 recruits received from Administrative Centre.	
	24/1/16		A Brigade practice Fire Alarm was held at Headquarters, the practice was well carried out and the supply of buckets and water was satisfactory.	
	24/1/16		A Brigade Practice night alarm was held, the alarm received at 10-35 pm. the first company was on parade by 11-25 pm. the last at 12-0pm.midnight, the Transport was on parade by 12-25 am.	
	25/1/16		A draft of 19 Recruits received from Adminsitrative Centre.	
	25/1/16		A draft of 19 Recruits " " "	
	28/1/16		A draft of 6 Recruits " " "	
	27/1/16		A draft of 2 Recruits " " "	
	28/1/16		A draft of 2 Recruits " " "	
	30/1/16		A Battalion Practice Alarm was held, the alarm was sent out at 10-40 am. by unmounted Orderlies the first Company was on parade at 11-12 am. the last at 11-19. Transport at 11-19 am.	

...................Lieut. Col.
Commanding
2/10th (Scottish) Battn. K. L. R.

2/10th(Scottish)Bn.L'pool Regt.

W A R   D I A R Y

for the month

of

FEBRUARY 1916.

Station :- MAIDSTONE, KENT.

Army Form C. 2118.

WAR DIARY
or
INTELLIGENCE SUMMARY

(Erase heading not required.)

Instructions regarding War Diaries and Intelligence Summaries are contained in F. S. Regs., Part II and the Staff Manual respectively. Title Pages will be prepared in manuscript.

Place	Date	Hour	Summary of Events and Information	Remarks and references to Appendices
Maidstone	4/2/16	0.30	An aerial observation post of 1 N.C.O. and 4 men was established at Otham at Stanacre Farm. Sec.Lieut. H.S. Bennett was appointed in charge of the posts at Hollingbourne, Otham and Linton.	
	24/2/16	0.30 0.30	The Battalion received orders to hold itself in readiness to move in case of an alarm. 15 recruits (group) were received during the month.	

Adam Gawne
.... Lt. Col.
Og. 2/10th (Scottish) Bn. The King's (L'pool Regt.)

www.ingramcontent.com/pod-product-compliance
Lightning Source LLC
Chambersburg PA
CBHW051528190426
43193CB00045BA/2657